CHICHESTER
IN OLD PHOTOGRAPHS

CHICHESTER
IN OLD PHOTOGRAPHS

COLLECTED BY
ROB HARMER

ALAN SUTTON

Alan Sutton Publishing Limited
Phoenix Mill · Far Thrupp · Stroud · Gloucestershire

First published 1990

British Library Cataloguing in Publication Data

Chichester in old photographs.
1. West Sussex. Chichester (District), history
I. Harmer, Rob *1928-*
942.262

ISBN 0-86299-801-8

Typset in 9/10 Korinna.
Typesetting and origination by
Alan Sutton Publishing Limited.
Printed in Great Britain by
Dotesios Printers Limited.

CONTENTS

A GARDEN FÊTE in 1908. Note the lanterns. This may have been taken in Oaklands Park.

INTRODUCTION

Chichester is a historic Roman city in south-west Sussex. There has been a Cathedral here for over one thousand years. Many traces of the Roman occupation have been found in the area including the great palace at Fishbourne which was probably built for the legate Cogidubnus. The remains were first discovered by workmen digging a trench in the fields while widening a road some thirty-five years ago. The arms and charter of the city were granted by Henry I and the mayor and Corporation have existed almost continuously since then.

The photographs I have chosen for inclusion, showing various aspects of city life over a period of about ninety years, will be new to most people. They begin at the Market Cross at the centre of intersecting streets, a busy crossroads complicated by buses having to use routes against the traffic. A point-duty policeman could be seen here at one time. It has been the place from which proclamations have traditionally been made, as the following photographs will show.

Within the city the open space of Priory Park was donated by the Duke of Richmond. Its Gala Day continues a tradition of carnivals and sports for in past years it has been used for Bank Holiday sports, cycle racing, children's entertainments, tennis tournaments, and for outdoor musical events such as "Merrie England" with Webster Booth and Anne Ziegler. The medieval Guildhall is within the park and nearby in St Martins Lane is St Mary's Hospital – a special home for the old and infirm since the thirteenth century.

A distinguishing feature of the cathedral is the detached bell-tower sometimes known as Ryman's Tower. The spire, which once fell, is 277 ft high making Chichester the only cathedral, it is said, which can be seen from the sea.

During the Civil War the city was besieged by Parliamentary troops who captured it for Cromwell in 1642. Some of the effects of the war may still be seen in the cathedral. William Cawley, a mayor, was a regicide who later fled to the European mainland. His name has been commemorated in Cawley almshouses, Cawley Road and Cawley Lodge.

Outside the city walls the scaffold for criminals sentenced to death was on the Broyle. News sheets of the time contain graphic accounts of these occasions. The smuggler's stone may still be seen near the Wellington Road corner of Broyle Road, by the barracks.

Chichester has long been a centre of government. The West Sussex County Council was formed in 1889 and the County Hall built in 1936. Before then council offices were housed in various buildings in the city. Local government has been a major employer as have the medical and nursing services, valuation offices, and Inland Revenue, among others. It has also been a communications centre for road, canal and rail, helping the flow of industrial and agricultural goods. An important market town, it held markets twice a week at one time. Before the cattle market was built these were held in the main streets. The corn exchange was in East Street. Important industries connected with farming included fleece preparation at the wool staplers, and corn and seed merchants.

Chichester is known as the Georgian city but many of the interesting small houses and cottages were in the Somerstown area outside the city walls, small back-to-back cottages with no bathrooms, built in the eighteenth and nineteenth centuries. Unfortunately these have been destroyed by modern planners. They were the homes of shoemakers and of people like Joseph Faro, the pieman, or little grocers shops, or pubs like the Beehive.

There are a number of small churches of great interest beside the Cathedral – St Olave's, St Andrew's and St John's for example. Some are still in use today as a shop or art gallery, but others have been destroyed or lie idle and in disuse. The Pallants area within the city was administered by the Archbishop of Canterbury. The word derives from the Latin *palentia* signifying an exclusive authority. The four Pallants were once the homes of professional men.

I hope the photographs in this selection provide a picture of Chichester life as it was lived and will appeal not only to established residents but also to more recent arrivals in the city.

The Cross and The Streets

Being a Roman city, Chichester's main streets are built on a typical pattern, with the four roads coming from the four cardinal points of the compass and meeting at a central point. West Street has had only a few shops and is mainly residential, with the Cathedral on its south side. At the centre stands the Market Cross built in 1500. Markets were held in East and North Streets at one time. Some archaeological excavations have been made over the years, although the 'Pudens Stone' of Roman origin was found accidentally by workmen in North Street in the eighteenth century.

THE CROSS before the railings were removed in 1872. To the right is the top of Henry Gambling, chemist and dentist.

THE CROSS. To the left of the Cross is Lennards Shoe Shop, No. 1 East Street. Also to the left in West Street No. 1, Panchen; No. 2, Singer Sewing Machines; No. 3, Cotterell; No. 4, Burkitt. In 1926 Southdown Motor Services had an office at No. 4.

JOE FARO AT THE CROSS. Joe was a baker and pieman. He is shown holding his portable pie oven, which he used at various pitches, including the cattle market, Sloe Fair and the Cross from 1863 to 1913. The pie oven survives in the Chichester District Museum.

NORTH STREET around 1910. Shops which may be seen are (on the left) No. 8, F.H. Washington; No. 9, Sidney Bastow (chemists); No. 10, Howard (photographers); No. 11, Jarman & Sons (grocers). On the opposite side is the sign, with three bats, of the sports dealers, G. Prew, (No. 82). Chichester Technical Institute (right) was built in 1900 to commemorate Queen Victoria's Diamond Jubilee.

NORTH STREET in the 1920s. The Council Chambers include the Assembly Rooms and the Mayor's Parlour.

THE WHEATSHEAF HOTEL, at No. 80 North Street c. 1905. At around that time E. Gosling was the landlord. In 1916 the building became Geerings, drapers and milliners.

NORTH STREET c. 1938. The edge of Bastow's, the chemist, Woolworth's (nothing over 6d.), and Andrews' cycle shop.

A VIEW OF NORTH STREET from the top of the Ship Hotel.

NORTH HOUSE HOTEL, No. 67 North Street. In 1908 this was a boarding house with proprietor A. Moody. From 1910–19 it was run by the Purchase family. In the 1920s it was owned by W. Burr. The hotel was originally owned by Major-General Parry.

ARTHUR PURCHASE'S WINE MERCHANTS, 32 North Street.

A PROCESSION FROM THE BARRACKS down Broyle Road, preceded by a Dunnaway taxi, an Argyll, known as the 'mustard pot'.

ON THE RIGHT is the shop of Messrs Harris & Hall, the Chichester Central Supply Stores, at Nos 2–3 East Street. A special room was provided for tea, one of their specialities.

EAST STREET. On the left are: No. 83, Lewis & Son, jewellers (formerly Wimhurst); No. 84, Reynolds, hosier; No. 86, Maypole, grocers; No. 87, Kimbell, butchers, specializing in bacon.

EAST STREET IN THE EDWARDIAN ERA. Many of the façades remain the same today.

SUMMERTIME IN EAST STREET earlier this century. Byerley's, fishmongers, is on the right. The printers, Willis & Co., is near the passageway leading to St Andrews church. Printing in East street had been carried on for over 100 years. Elphicks the butchers is on the left.

EAST STREET C. 1905. On the left is the Corn Exchange, built in 1833 with later alterations. Many local societies use it for various purposes including flower shows, choral competitions and amateur dramatics. At one time it was used as a cinema and professional theatre. Bransby Williams played here in the 1920s, and Mrs 'Willie' James from West Dean produced plays.

CARRIAGES in East Street around 1900.

SOUTH STREET in the 1920s. On the left is Canon Gate, then No. 24a, R. Allen, jewellers; No. 23, Bunting, tobacconist, (later Bartholomew); No. 22, S.J. Linkins, saddler & sports goods; No. 20, Styles, confectioner, and No. 19, F.M. Barber, fishmonger.

ON THE RIGHT SIDE OF SOUTH STREET No. 44 is the Regnum Club, No. 46, Wimhurst, No. 47, Fleetwood, No. 49, T.F. Lummus, the King's Head and the post office.

SOUTH STREET in the 1930s. This picture shows Lewis's, on the left, which was the old theatre, the Regnum Club. At this time parking was allowed on the sides of the street; which side varied according to whether the day's date was odd or even.

West Street, Chichester

WEST STREET. The railings beside the Cathedral were taken down in 1941 to provide metal for the war effort.

WEST STREET, c. 1905.

THE DOLPHIN HOTEL YARD, West Street.

THE BUS STATION in West Street, looking west from the top of the Cross on 1 December 1944. Buses include No. 31 (Southsea to Brighton) and No. 52 (Summersdale to Selsey). Other vehicles are shown with their wartime covered headlights.

Westgate, Chichester 60566

AN EARLY POSTCARD OF WESTGATE. Eric Gill, artist and sculptor, lived nearby at No. 2 North Walls.

EASTGATE SQUARE AND EAST STREET with archway and decorations probably for Queen Victoria's Diamond Jubilee in 1897. On the right are G. Barnes, poulterer, and Sharp Garland's shop.

SHARP GARLAND'S STORES, Eastgate Square, between 1910 and 1920. The building was said to be unsafe and was demolished in 1964.

NORTH WALLS. This view shows the steps down towards Tower Street and The Grange, later demolished and replaced by the County Hall.

A VICTORIAN VIEW OF THE WALLS.

NORTH WALLS, c. 1920.

NORTH WALLS, near Tower Street, where there was a Gothic Revival house, The Grange, a successor to the medieval Grange occupied by the Dean of Chichester.

EAST WALLS – THE ROMAN WALL. On the right are the buildings of the YMCA and the factory of Shippam Ltd.

Royal Celebrations and Events

Chichester has had visits by Kings and Queens from Elizabeth I to our present Queen. Royal visits have been made to St Mary's Hospital, various shops and Shippam's Ltd. Proclamations of royal accessions, deaths, etc. have been made from the Market Cross on the East Street side. Diamond Jubilees and Coronations have been celebrated by processions and events in Priory Park.

A PROCESSION WITH THE MAYOR AND CORPORATION OF THE CITY outside the Cathedral for the wedding of Lady Doris Lennox, daughter of the 7th Duke of Richmond. She was married on 10 April 1923 to Mr Clare Vyner, son of Lord and Lady Alwyn Compton of Newby Hall, Ripon, North Yorkshire. Lady Doris died in 1980. Charles II bestowed the title of Richmond on Louise Keraulle, one of his mistresses.

EAST STREET. Putting up decorations for an early twentieth-century coronation, either that of Edward VII or George V. Photographed by J.W. Barnes of the Chichester Photographic Society.

THE CROSS. The mayor reading the proclamation for Queen Victoria's Golden Jubilee in 1887.

THE PROCLAMATION AT THE CROSS of the accession of Queen Elizabeth II on 7 February 1952. The Mayor, Russell Purchase; the Dean, the Very Revd Arthur Duncan Jones and the Revd Godfrey Wells (with medals and an eye-patch) of the Subdeanery can be seen.

THE PROCLAMATION announcing the accession of King George V.

THE PROCLAMATION AT THE CROSS of the death of King George V in January 1936.

THE PROCLAMATION OF THE DEATH OF KING GEORGE VI, who died on 6 February 1952.

CORONATION DAY IN SOUTH STREET, probably King George V's in 1911. The City Corporation procession may be seen.

SOUTH STREET decorated for the celebrations of the 1935 Silver Jubilee of George V and Queen Mary. On the right is the post office and the Plaza cinema.

EAST STREET decorated for the Coronation of Queen Elizabeth II, June 1953.

ROBERT ALLEN, at No. 24a South Street. This picture shows Queen Mary's visit in 1929.

QUEEN MARY window shopping at Robert Allen's in South Street in 1929!

SECTION THREE

The Cathedral
and the Church

The Cathedral has dominated the city since its foundation in the twelfth century. In Victorian times the spire fell down and recently much work has been required to rebuild and restore the walls and buttresses of Caen stone. The Cathedral has had great influence on the City and the south-west quadrant in particular, occupied as it is by the Deanery, Bishop's Palace, and the houses of the clergy in St Richard's Walk and Canon Lane. The smaller churches, – St Olave's, for example – are not neglected either.

CHICHESTER CATHEDRAL from the south-east. To the right are the houses in Cawley Road. Note the corn stooks in the field.

FOLLOWING A PERIOD OF ANXIETY about its safety, Chichester Cathedral spire fell down at 1.30 p.m. on 16 February 1861. No one was injured as the building had been evacuated. The rebuilding began almost immediately.

A PEACEFUL SCENE on the Westgate Fields before any buildings and the ring-road were built. The fields went right up to the Roman walls.

THIS PICTURE SHOWS THE BISHOP'S PALACE which dates from the twelfth century, but has a thirteenth-century kitchen and a fifteenth-century hall.

ST RICHARD'S WALK, in the cathedral precincts. The Treasury, No. 2, was built in 1834, replacing older residences.

MR HORACE ARTHUR HAWKINS (1880–1966). He was appointed cathedral organist from 1938–58 upon his retirement from Hurstpierpoint College.

THE BELL TOWER built in the late four-teenth or early fifteenth century. It con-tains a peal of eight bells. The hours were struck on a bell weighing 74 cwt. known as 'Big Walter'.

CHICHESTER CATHEDRAL CHOIR. The Choir School in 1930. Back row, left to right: Mr Lumley, -?-, -?-, ? Moore, Mr Moore, Will Rowe, Mr Osborne, Joseph Wilkins, Harry Whitehouse, Revd D. Manners. Second row: John Marks, -?-, Dennis Ayling, Mr Ball (headmaster, Northgate Choir School), Mr Clarke, Kenneth Wells, ? Knights, Raymond Chatters. Third row: Victor Halsey, Frederick Hilton, ? Ayling, Dr M.P. Conway (organist, 1925–31), Gerald Twort, Tony Dobson, Ray Hillsden. Front row: Roy Pend (?), Ronald West, Raymond Dobson, Pat Francis.

MR E.J. MARSHALL, headmaster of Brighton Grammar School (1861–99). He was born at the Central School in New Park Road on 9 September 1832, later living at Barnham. He can be seen at the right of the group of boys in the bottom picture.

A GROUP OF BRIGHTON GRAMMAR SCHOOL BOYS on the top of the cathedral tower in the 1880s. One of the boys is possibly the famous illustrator Aubrey Beardsley who attended the school at about this time.

THE BISHOP OF CHICHESTER, the Rt. Revd George K.A. Bell, leading a procession of clergy at the dedication of the Coronation window in the Cathedral on 13 June, 1953. Following the bishop is the chaplain of the theological college, Revd James Hannon, and the Archbishop of Canterbury, the Rt. Revd and Rt. Hon. Geoffrey Fisher. This event also commemorated the seventh centenary of St Richard.

THE ARCHBISHOP OF CANTERBURY with Mrs Fisher and the bishops of Chichester and Lewes on the occasion of the unveiling of the Coronation window.

A VISIT BY QUEEN MARY, probably in 1929.

A PROCESSION PASSING WREN HOUSE, West Street, in the 1930s. The occasion was the visit of prelates of the Greek Orthodox Church.

60869

St. Bartholomew's Church, Chichester

ST BARTHOLOMEW'S CHURCH was called the Church of St Sepulchre until the reign of Henry VIII. During the siege in the Civil War in 1642 it was destroyed and was finally rebuilt in 1832.

THE FUNERAL OF RT. REVD ERNEST ROLAND WILBERFORCE, Bishop of Chichester, 14 September 1927.

BISHOP WILBERFORCE.

ST MARY'S HOSPITAL. The chapel is thirteenth-century. The large east window was blown out in the Second World War, but a replacement was made by Christopher Webb.

St. Mary's Hospital, Chichester
Published by W. H. Barrett, The Cross, Chichester

ST MARY'S HOSPITAL. The roof of the chapel, in the extreme right of the picture, has remained unchanged since the fourteenth century. It has a pitch of 42 ft.

A VISIT TO ST MARY'S HOSPITAL in 1908 by King Edward VII and Queen Alexandra, before they went on to Goodwood races. The King had made a previous visit in 1906, and promised to bring the Queen with him next time. Every resident was seen, the oldest present being Miss Redman, aged 89.

PORTFIELD CHURCH in Cemetery Lane, designed in thirteenth-century style and consecrated in 1871.

Trades and Business

Many businesses have thrived in the city on account of its position as a commercial centre in south-west Sussex. Some of these businesses have been connected with agriculture and farming: wool preparation, corn and seed merchants, tanneries and agricultural engineers. Shops prospered – some, like Shippam's fish and meat products for example, have become known nationally. The needles made in the cottages in the St Pancras area were known before the Civil War and used throughout England.

People from a wide local area often came once a week to visit the numerous shops, the butchers, drapers, grocers, tobacconists and sweet shops, not forgetting the many public houses in the city.

CHICHESTER COAL CO., 34a Southgate, owned by A.F. Lewis. A young Mervyn Cutten stands in the doorway.

NO. 79 EAST STREET, formerly William Byles, then Mrs J. Byles, wine merchant and wholesale tallow chandler. William Hounson Byles was an artist. Born on 1 December 1870 he died 11 February 1928. Behind these premises was, at one time, a little bar called The Rifleman. It had no windows!

HOWARD'S THE BUTCHERS, in North Street. From left to right: Oswald Collins (manager), son of Frank Collins; Richard Collins (1851–1937) of Barnham; Charlie Howard; Dick Joyce; Bill Rapson.

GEORGE PHILLIPS. Grocer, wine and spirit merchant, The Hornet.

TUPPER'S GENERAL STORES of No. 14 St Pancras.

G.H. PESKETT, tailors, No. 55 East Street from about 1916. Previously the premises of W. Hart, gunmaker.

MESSRS JOHN LENG & SONS, St Pancras, near Eastgate Square. The firm was established in 1824, trading in genuine antique furniture. Queen Mary visited the shop in 1929.

PENNEYS. Drapers of No. 73 North Street, close to the Assembly Rooms.

THE THIRD CHARLES SHIPPAM. He built up the business first started by his grandfather (also Charles), who opened a grocery shop in Westgate in 1786. In 1897 he was succeeded by his five sons in partnership.

SHIPPAM'S FIRST FACTORY, built at the time of the third Charles Shippam in 1892, behind No. 47 East Street. This enabled the company to start producing potted meat and fish paste.

SHIPPAM'S new factory in East walls C. 1914.

A TRADE CARD of around 1890 for Shippam's famous sausages.

EAST STREET DECORATIONS — probably for Queen Victoria's Diamond Jubilee in 1897. Shippam's shop is to the left of the Swan Inn. The office of Mr Budden, the builder, is to the right.

THE SHIPPAM FACTORY WORKS OUTING in 1925. The first charabanc was built in 1923, Type Tilling-Stevens T 53.

A GROUP OF WORKMEN, probably in about 1910.

WORKERS OUTSIDE EBENEZER PRIOR LTD, woolstaplers, in Tower Street in the late 1920s.

THE MAN WITH THE HOD is Henry Hall who lived at Hall's Court, Tower Street.

EAST PALLANT. The Pallants were called 'a little city within the city'. At the intersection of the roads was a wooden cross, but it was destroyed in 1713. The tanners and curriers used to take their leather there to be stamped by an official to prove that it was of satisfactory quality.

EAST ROW in the 1930s. Sadler & Co., corn merchants, transferring sacks at their grain store (now Chichester District Museum).

EAST ROW in the 1930s. Sadler & Co.'s lorry is being unloaded into a hayloft.

MARKET DAY, this view looks towards Eastgate Square.

Education

Education has always been important in the city, with schools like Oliver Whitby and the Prebendal in West Street, the Victorian central schools and the Lancastrian schools for boys and girls, some private schools such as St John's and, of course, Chichester Grammar School. Later in the twentieth century came the advent of Chichester High Schools for Girls and Boys.

CHICHESTER HIGH SCHOOL FOR GIRLS, Stockbridge Road, in 1910. The school was opened on 22 September 1909. The cost of the building was £8,888.

LINDENAU SCHOOL 22/3 North Street. The principal was Miss A.M. Pearce.

THIS APPEARS TO BE ST PANCRAS JUNIOR SCHOOL at some time between 1911 and 1913.

THE CENTRAL GIRLS' SCHOOL, Chapel Street.

RICHARD FORDER, who was an Oliver Whitby boy. Oliver Whitby's school was founded under the terms of his will in 1702. It was situated in West Street, rebuilt in 1904–5, and closed in 1950.

THE WHYKE INFANTS FÊTE in The Whyke Vicarage garden, which was on the west side of Whyke Road. It was between Cleveland Road and Cambrai Avenue.

FORM 1B in the chemistry laboratory at Chichester High School for Boys, July 1940. Front row, left to right: D. Makeham (side of face only), Roy Macey, Derek Longlands,? Wyatt, J. Wickham. Second row: D. Strange, Stan Hanwell, Rob Harmer,? Hoad,? Groves. Third row: J.H.B. Smith, ? Snelling, B. Ordish, L. Eyears, N. Gunning, E. Culverwell. Fourth row: ? White, D. Waters, -?-, ? Bell, -?-, Dudley Smith (now Sir and an MP). Fifth row: W.H. Clayton, M. Hughes, M. Sparkes.

AN EARLY PICTURE of Bishop Otter College, c. 1880, the training college for teachers.

GIRLS WITH THEIR CYCLES from Bishop Otter College in College Lane (at one time called Love Lane).

A HOCKEY MATCH on the sports field of Bishop Otter College.

TEACHING PRACTICE. A student from the Bishop Otter training course for teachers, c. 1910.

THE LANCASTRIAN SCHOOL SPORTS. The photograph was by D.W. Baker of No. 5 Cleveland Road.

SECTION SIX

Events and the Social Scene

The city with its various facilities – parks, hotels and assembly rooms – was the central point for many organizations. Summer events in Priory and Oaklands Parks have been enjoyed by many, along with the more formal occasions at the Cathedral, mayor-making ceremonies, and civic receptions.

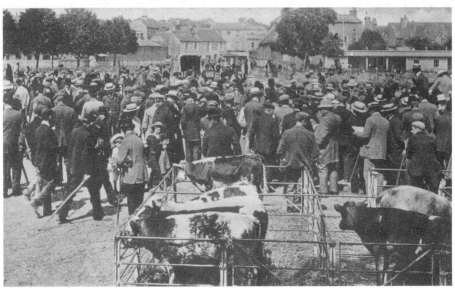

MARKET DAY at the Cattle Market, looking towards Eastgate Square between 1880 and 1900. At this time Market Day was as much a social as a commercial occasion.

THE SLOE FAIR in the 1890s, showing Joseph Matthew's roundabout. The fair began in the reign of Henry I with a grant to Ralph, Bishop of Chichester in 1107/8. The name 'Sloe' derives from the sloe tree which stood in the field near the Northgate where the fair has been held for centuries.

PRIORY PARK came under the ownership of the Duke of Richmond in 1824. In 1918 Priory Park was given to the city as a war memorial by the 7th Duke of Richmond.

ANOTHER VIEW OF PRIORY PARK early on in the 1900s.

THE SECOND ANNUAL POLICE SPORTS DAY of West Sussex Constabulary, held in Priory Park on 16 July 1914.

A PRESENTATION IN PRIORY PARK. The event is not known, but possibly it took place in the 1920s.

THE FOURTEENTH ANNUAL CYCLING SPORTS held in Priory Park on Whitsun Bank Holiday, 22 May 1893. The event of the day was the three miles scratch cycle race for the President's Challenge Badge. It was won for the second time by Mr J.D. Foster in 8 min. 47⅕ sec. The winner received the badge from the mayor, Sir Robert Raper.

THE ALEXANDRA ROSE DAY FÊTE in Priory Park on 25 June 1914. The motor cycle and side-car musical chairs was won by H. Osborn and Miss Ballard. The city band played under the baton of Mr H. Brodie, and ladies sold wild roses in the streets (like the cornflowers in more recent times). The funds collected were for the benefit of the Royal West Sussex Hospital.

ARCHIE BAKER AS OLD MOTHER HUBBARD. He was the first prize winner in a costume event at the Whit Monday sports in Priory Park, 1893.

THE CHICHESTER CITY GUARD was formed at a meeting at the Assembly Rooms on 13 August 1914, chaired by the mayor, Sharp Garland, and by Admiral Holland. Volunteer Civil Guards in West Sussex were called for by the Chief Constable on 11 August to help with security and the checking of aliens. The Chichester Guard had its first drill on 17 August by the Guildhall in Priory Park. The Commandant appointed was Capt. Gibbings of North Street and 150 men attended. Admiral Holland lived at Langley House in West Street.

Residential Areas and Hospitals

Chichester has gradually spread out from the city walls, small cottages and terraced housing growing up in areas like St Pancras and Somerstown, although many of the streets had large houses for the notable. In the late-Victorian period development began in the Melbourne Road area and beyond the Hornet, in the parish of Whyke and Portfield. There are fewer old photographs and postcards of these residential areas but pictures taken by amateur photographers of the early twentieth century do sometimes turn up.

Hospitals were provided for the aged and infirm and for the sick both in body and mind. They included the isolation hospital in Spitalfield Lane, the Graylingwell mental hospital, and the West Sussex County Hospital in Broyle Road.

TOWER STREET in the early 1920s. The house covered with creeper belonged to Ebenezer Prior. Hall's Court, the home of Mr and Mrs Hall is situated in the middle of the terrace.

A VIEW TOWARDS THE CATHEDRAL from Tower Street.

TOWER STREET in the twenties, showing the Jannece ice cream barrow. The lady standing by the drain-pipe is Mrs Tidy. Her husband was well-known for repairing china by riveting. The Greenshields children, Joan, Tom, Archie and Kenneth are standing near the barrow, with Dorothy Hall on the left.

THE BOYS' SUSSEX CENTRAL SCHOOL was opened in November 1812, on a site called The Bishop's Garden. The central schools owe their origin to the Rt. Revd John Buckner, Bishop of Chichester 1798–1824. The girls' school was founded in 1884 in Chapel Street, and the infants' in Tower Street in 1896. This building was demolished in the 1880s and then rebuilt for the Boys' Central School.

NEW PARK ROAD in the parish of St Pancras, known at one time as Litten Road.

MELBOURNE ROAD, probably in the 1920s. On the left is A.M. Green, grocer and post office, and in the background Pink's soda water factory.

SNOW DRIFTS in Green Lane, 30 December 1908.

GREEN LANE around 1910.

A VIEW TAKEN BEFORE THE DEVELOPMENT OF KINGSHAM ROAD AND STIRLING ROAD. The footpath is no longer in existence.

WHYKE at the turn of the century.

CHICHESTER ASSEMBLY ROOMS. J.W. Loader Cooper, Town Clerk, and Alderman G. Turnbull were admitted as Freemen of the City on 7 June 1934.

WEST SUSSEX HOSPITAL during the 1890s. Note the small tree and the wisteria which later covered the whole façade.

WEST SUSSEX HOSPITAL, CHICHESTER

THE WISTERIA, which became a feature covering the whole of the font of the hospital, can be seen in this photograph of c. 1900.

(I)

RE-OPENING OF ROL W. SUSSEX HOSPITAL CHICHESTER BY H. M THE KING AUG 2/13 CHICHESTER

THE RE-OPENING OF WEST SUSSEX HOSPITAL performed by King George V on 2 August 1913. In honour of the occasion it was renamed the Royal West Sussex Hospital. On the left can be seen the 7th Duke of Richmond (with beard).

DR DAVID EWART presenting prizes to nurses at the hospital. Dr Ewart lived at No. 31 North Street, and had a surgery in Guildhall Street.

ANNA SEWELL, author of *Black Beauty* lived here *c.* 1856 with her parents, Isaac and Mary. Her father was manager of the Capital and Counties Bank in East Street.

THE PATIENTS' GARDEN at Graylingwell Hospital. Graylingwell opened in July 1897 as the West Sussex Mental Hospital, and was enlarged in 1901.

GRAYLINGWELL became a war casualty hospital during the First World War. This is the staff of KE 2 ward.

NEW HOUSES being built in Whyke (possibly Hay Road), 19 February 1946.

SECTION EIGHT

The Wars

Chichester has had its share of war throughout the centuries: in 1642 the city was beseiged by Parliamentary troops; possible French invasion prompted the building of the barracks in the city; the Royal Sussex Regiment were based here for many years, sending out battalions to the Boer War as well as the later World Wars. Some bombing took place here during the course of the Second World War and RAF Tangmere, being very near the city (with its satellite airfields) reminded inhabitants of our own aerial activities. St James' School and Bishop Otter College were used as emergency operations rooms.

THE VERY REVD DEAN I. HANNAH dedicating the war memorial on its original site in Eastgate Square. Later the memorial was moved to the Litten in St Pancras.

THE BRITISH TANK, a Female Mk 2 and a German artillery gun on display in Priory Road. The gun was presented to the city in 1920 by the Royal Sussex Regiment who had captured it during the First World War. The Roman wall can be seen behind them.

A PEACE CELEBRATION outside the Guildhall, Priory Park, Chichester 1919. Seated to the right of the mayor is the 7th Duke of Richmond.

A FIRST-WORLD-WAR BRITISH TANK was presented to the city on 29 September 1919. After a procession, headed by a volunteer bugle band, the City Corporation stood on the tank outside the Corn Exchange when the mayor (Sharp Garland) made his speech of acceptance.

CHICHESTER BARRACKS, the home of the Royal Sussex Regiment. In 1803 wooden huts were constructed by French prisoners, with additions in 1854, 1861, 1874 and 1881. The Militia Field was outside the South Gate and a stone marks the spot where two smugglers were hanged in 1785.

THE RETURN OF SOLDIERS FROM THE SOUTH AFRICAN (BOER) WAR, which ended in July 1902.

A STREET PARTY IN LITTLE LONDON celebrating the end of the war in Europe on VE Day. Violet is on the extreme left holding her son, Leonard. Mrs Alice Atkins, holding a tea-cup, is her mother. Families include Talbot, Williams, Luff, Turner and Denyer.

THE CAVALRY RIDING BY in St Pancras. The coachworks of Messrs Cutton Bros is on the right. James Ewer Cutten was mayor of St Pancras in 1828. Upon the death of William Cobden in July 1837 he served out as mayor. He was appointed Town Clerk of St Pancras in 1843.

ST PANCRAS DECORATED FOR A SPECIAL OCCASION. Note the carts on the left.

The St Pancras Corporation

The Corporation of St Pancras, complete with its own mayor, began in 1689 following the accession of William and Mary. It still exists today with its own mace and mayor's insignia and functions as a charity institution supporting the poor and needy. The Corporation elects its mayor every November and has an annual dinner. It is believed that this 'mock mayor' is now the only one surviving in the country.

ST PANCRAS CORPORATION MEMBERS outside the Unicorn on Christmas Day, 1911. From left to right: Percy Lewis, Sam Baker, W.P. Breach (mace bearer), George Cover, George Kemp and Davis Cover.

CORPORATION OF ST PANCRAS LEAVING HDQRS WITH XMAS DINNERS. 3

THE CORPORATION OF ST PANCRAS delivered Christmas Day dinners to the old people in Dear's Almshouses in the Hornet.

CORPORATION OF ST PANCRAS AT THE ALMSHOUSES ON XMAS DAY. 4.

PANCRAS CORPORATION XMAS DINNER 1918. MOREY PHOTO 3.

ST PANCRAS CORPORATION delivering Christmas dinners in 1918 to the ladies in Dear's Almshouses. Miss Dear had left £1,000, the interest from which was to be applied to repairing the building, the balance, if any, to be divided among the four ladies. They would possibly receive about £6 per year.

THE CORPORATION OF ST PANCRAS, 21 July 1910, at Ivy Bank, home of city mayor, Sharp Garland.

A GARDEN PARTY given by the Mayor of St Pancras, John Sewell Courtauld (MP for Chichester) for the Burgesses of St Pancras Corporation and their wives. It was held at Burton Park, near Petworth, 26 July 1928. Back row, left to right: George Lewis, -?-, J. Plumest (?), S.A. Ingrey, M. McNeil, H.C. Slaney, H.D. Ablewhite, Ernest Cutten, B. Pannel, G.S. Gould, S. Hillman, -?-, -?-, R.T. Willis, Laurie Cover, Jessie Cover, A.J. Flanagan, F.B. Tomkins, William Jones. Middle row: -?-, -?-, Charlie Hooker, Mrs P. Lewis, Percy Lewis, Lydia Cutten, -?-, R.V. Weare, -?-, H.J. Morgan, -?-, -?-, A. Phillips, H. Turner, T. Lummus, -?-, G.F. Bevis, -?-, -?-, Maud O'Flanagan, -?-, -?-. Front row: P.T. Wingham, Mrs Wingham, -?-, -?-, H.R. Cutten, Mrs Cover, G. Cover, D. Kimbell, Mrs Coutauld, Major J.S. Courtauld (mayor), W.P. Bleach, J.W. Loader Cooper, -?-, -?-. Seated on the lawn: G. Kemp, C.C. Allen, Mrs Allen, Mrs Smithers, -?-, G.A. Smithers.

MEMBERS OF THE ST PANCRAS CORPORATION outside the Unicorn in Eastgate Square on 6 May 1935 – the Silver Jubilee of King George V and Queen Mary. Back row: two onlookers, George Phillips, -?-, -?-, Tom Kimbell, Cyril Flowers, Sid Cover, T. Humphreys, Sam Horner, Theo Parkin, R. Sykes, -?-, G. Kemp, -?-. Front row: R. Willmer, Albert Flanagan, -?-, H.D. Ablewhite, George Cover, David Kimbell, W.D. Breach, -?-, -?-.

Personalities

This small section concentrates on those who have been well-known in the city of Chichester and includes the pieman at the Cross, Joe Faro.

WILLIAM JOSEPH SHAYER (1811–92), born in Chichester and well-known for his coaching paintings. His uncle was William Combes who ran the independent post coach from the Anchor to London.

A MILL AT BIRDHAM, photographed in 1929. The corn milled here was probably sent to Sadlers Ltd of Chichester. The miller was possibly William Farne.

PORTFIELD MILL with its last millers, the Stovels, before its demolition between 1900 and 1905. Diamond Cottage can be seen on the right. The sails were traditionally set as shown on the occasion of a wedding or funeral in the miller's family.

THE PRINCE AND PRINCESS OF SAXE-WEIMAR with members of Chichester Corporation. The Prince had married Augusta Catherine, daughter of the 5th Duke of Richmond. He died on 16 November 1902 and is buried in the Richmond vault in the cathedral.

ADOLPHUS BALLARD, Mayor of the City of Chichester, 1896 and 1897, shown in his mayoral robes for the 1897 Diamond Jubilee of Queen Victoria. He lived at No. 5 East Pallant, and carried on an ironmonger's business at No. 6–8 East Street.

AMELIA IDLE, née Collins (10 March 1798 to 2 June 1879), worked at Charges, the draper by the Cross, and eloped with an officer from the Chichester barracks. Many years later she returned to her native Bosham and lived until about 1870 at Church Farm and then at Shopwyke Hall where she died. She was buried in Portfield churchyard.

JAMES H. FARO outside his home at No. 50 George Street, Somerstown. He is wearing his baker's hat and apron and is holding a portable pie oven. His son, Joseph N. Faro, was a railway ticket collector. He committed suicide on the railway line between Cawley and Snag's Lane Crossings, on 7 December 1892.

LITTLE LONDON. The name was purportedly given to the area by Elizabeth I when visiting the city. Here are the old newspaper offices and works of R.J. Acford.

THE HOARE FAMILY, father and sons, behind No. 10 Caledonian Road. From left to right: Reg (railway clerk), Ted (wearing Oliver Whitby school uniform), Alfred (father, post office worker), Edward (post office worker, telegrams).

THE POST OFFICE IN SOUTH STREET, showing the staff standing outside. These premises were specially built in 1891, giving enough room for a sorting office, thus causing the one formerly used at the railway station to fall into disuse. When the post office moved to West Street in 1937, the County Library Headquarters moved in to this building.

THE FUNERAL OF MR EUGENE E. STREET, JP, FSA, of St Martins House, St Martins, on 17 October 1913. He was secretary to the Infirmary, a Liberal agent, Hon. Curator of the former Chichester Institute, and a supporter of the St John Ambulance. He died at the age of sixty-six.

THE LADIES OF THE WOMENS' HOUR of the South Street Wesleyan Methodist church in the early 1930s.

AN UNKNOWN OCCASION, probably dating from the 1920s. This is possibly the local MP, Major J.S. Courtauld MC.

Sport and Recreation

Association football has been played in various of the city's parks and recreation grounds; rugby in a field in the Hornet; cricket in Priory Park by many, both professional and amateur. Among the club names to be remembered are Chichester Ivanhoe and Gilbertians. Other sports included here are archery, tennis, bowls, athletics and cycling as well as bank holiday sports.

THE CORN EXCHANGE FOOTBALL CLUB was formed in September 1922, and played matches on Thursdays (early closing day, so tradesmen could play), and began the season with a 5–0 win over St Pauls. Ray Fielder is bottom left, sitting cross-legged. Players during this first season included: H. Ellis, G. Brewer, L. Smith, A. Adams, P. Smith, C.H. Crane, W. Dudman. Brewer and Crane also played for Chichester City 1st XI.

A TENNIS TOURNAMENT in Priory Park.

PRIORY PARK TENNIS CLUB. From left to right: P. Wills, ? Doman, H.R. Cutten, G. Cover.

THE OPENING MEETING, on an Easter Monday, of the Chichester and District Motor Cycle Club.

THERE WERE TWO GYMNASIUMS in the 1890s. One in East Street at the YMCA and the other in South Street/South Pallant. The gymnast on the left is Mr Sid Combes.

A GROUP OF CYCLISTS OUTSIDE THE ANCHOR in West Street on 2 May 1889. They belong to the Chichester and District Cyclists' Club.

THE YMCA GYMNASIUM was opened on 10 January 1892 by the mayor, Sir Robert Raper. A gymnastic display was given by members who were trained by staff instructor Cpl. Croley of the Royal Sussex Regimental Depot.

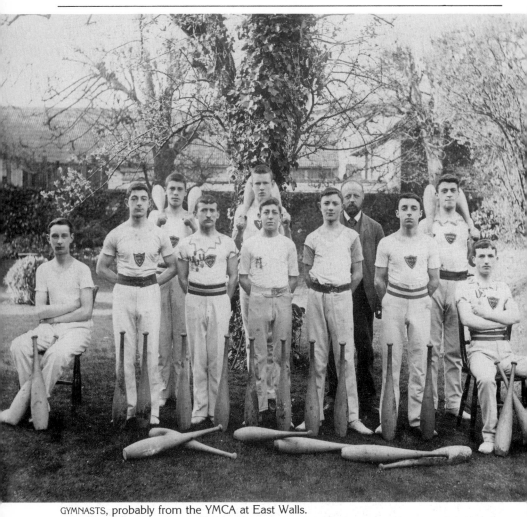

GYMNASTS, probably from the YMCA at East Walls.

CHICHESTER THURSDAYS FC, c. 1947. Back row, left to right: C. Dowling, -?-, B. Arnell, I. Gunning, G. Kewell, F. Forder. Front row: J. Mullinder, G. Stares, P. Fielder, A. Newton, E. Sellick.

COUNTY HALL SPORTS DAY, 1950, at the County Hall Sports Ground, Fishbourne Road. The County Hall Sports and Fête was held at the Old Whitby's former sports ground. At the 'Chinese laundry hoopla' stall is the chairman of the County Council, Sir Herbert Shiner (throwing), watched by Mr T.C. Hayward, the Clerk. The stall was organized by Sheila Heal (in the picture) and Audrey Newman. Two hundred people attended, the profit was £10.

THE COUNTY HALL SPORTS DAY 1950, ladies sack race. The race was won by Miss D. Long, Miss J. Chase was second and Miss D. Vine was third.

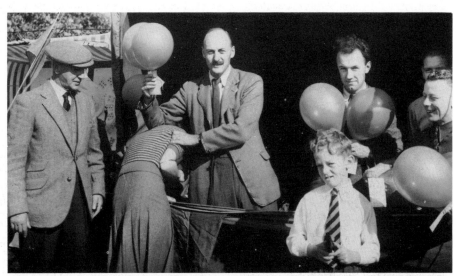

A BALLOON RACE at the County Hall Sports Day and Fête on 9 September 1950. The winner was Miss S. Scotcher of No. 1 Barford Road, whose balloon was found by Herr Adam Spilger II, of Rimbach Im Oldenwald, near Mannheim, Germany. John Ruffell (Planning department) and Bill Macey (Valuers department) with the balloons.

Transport

The bringing in of agricultural produce to the area and the carrying of coal, coke, etc. demanded various forms of transport. Depicted here are reminders of the coming of the omnibus and coach, the railway and the canal. In October of every year when the Sloe Fair took place the showmen's engines would assemble at the Cross before moving off in procession on the eve of the Fair with their wagons.

A SERENE PICTURE OF THE CHICHESTER CANAL. The chimney was a part of the buildings of the coal and coke merchants and contractors, Harry W. Harris & Co.

CHICHESTER CANAL with the gasworks and Cathedral in the background.

DUNNAWAY TAXIMEN outside the Portfield cemetery c. 1949. James and Richard Dunnaway with Jack Gadd.

CHICHESTER TAXI DRIVERS, Mr John Pulley-bank and Mr E. Dunnaway.

ERNEST DUNNAWAY outside Howard's Shop in Little London, c. 1931. The street was made one way in 1952–3.

ERNEST DUNNAWAY in 1957.

A CHARABANC OUTING by Priors, the woolstaplers. In the rear can be seen Mr and Mrs Mullinder and Mr and Mrs Combes.

THE FLEET OF MOTOR BUSES RUN BY W.G. DOWLE, trading as Summersdale Motor Services. He sold out to Southdown in January 1924 and became their first Chichester manager. The buses are BP 5177, a 14-seat Ford T; BP 7489, a 24-seat Vulcan; BP 8429, a 21-seat Vulcan. It is said that when signalled Dowle's buses would stop for anyone, but not for train passengers at Singleton station.

A LEYLAND TIGER TS4 in West Street outside the Southdown bus office. It had been derequisitioned and returned to the Southdown company in August 1946.

A VULCAN BUS photographed outside the bus garage in Northgate. It was acquired by Southdown with the business of W.G. Dowle, who traded as Summersdale Motor Service. Dowle then became Southdown's first Chichester manager.

A FRENCH-BUILT MORS, used for the first bus service between Bognor and Chichester in April 1907.

A SOUTHDOWN BUS with signboards for the route to Littlehampton, Worthing and Brighton – the No. 31 route.

THE FIRST TRAIN about to leave Chichester on the 'Selsey Tramway' in 1897. Some of the crowd at the opening ceremony are watching from the gasworks roof. Alderman Ballard, the mayor, climbed on board the locomotive *Chichester*, sounded the whistle and the train pulled out, but arrived at Selsey forty minutes late.

CHICHESTER STATION for the Selsey tramway (The old main line station building is in the background). The light railway opened in 1897 and closed in 1935.

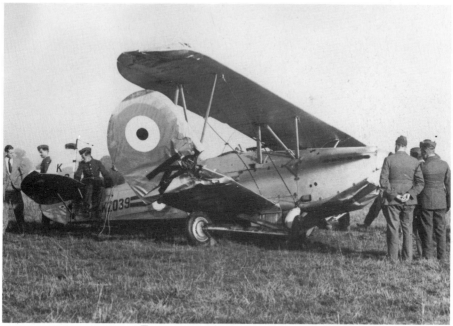

THE FAMOUS RAF AIRFIELD at Tangmere is the home of Nos. 1 and 43 fighter squadrons. During the thirties Hawker Furies were flown; these were replaced in 1938 by Hawker Hurricanes. The above shows a Hawker Fury Mark 1, K2039, of No. 1 squadron being inspected for damage on the south side of the airfield after a 'prang'.

A FODEN 4-TON WAGON with tipper gear owned by J.W.T. Heaver of Ratham, near Chichester from 1910 to 1915. It was probably on hire to Lewis & Co., from Heaver. Alf Kewell, Alf Elliott and George Edwards are seen standing by the wagon.

A FODEN 5-TON WAGON, Works No. 4194, built in 1913, registration M 5738, last licenced by Farr in 1923. It is shown at Farr's depository garage at the corner of St Pancras and Spitalfield Lane.

CARTHORSES AND WAGON in the early 1900s, possibly in Brandy Hole Lane, clearing wood from the copse.

A RENAULT CAR with four passengers in the lane to Goodwood.

The Fire and Police Services

The Chichester Fire Brigade and the West Sussex Constabulary were here long before their amalgamation into their respective country forces. The policeman was controlled by the traffic around the Cross were very well-known, as were the fireman who once had their engines by the market. The police station, once at Eastgate near the prison, later moved to South Street at Southgate. The police station was built and opened prior to the Second World War in Basin Road.

CHICHESTER CITY FIRE BRIGADE in front of their steam fire pump in the 1920s.

THE FIRE BRIGADE STEAM PUMP working in Eastgate Square. Pesketts, the tailors shown in the background, traded in the square until 1916.

THE WEST SUSSEX CONSTABULARY, for the first time at the July 1936 meeting of Goodwood Races, had no assistance from other police forces. The policemen pictured are: Sgt. Morris with PCs Baker, Chappel and Dunkley. The signature 'Friedrich' was signed by Friedrich of Prussia for PC Baker.

CHICHESTER POLICE, 1938. PC John Smith (bicycle), PC Roy Baker (motor cycle), PC George Brown (on horseback), PC Joe Coopey (standing). Just visible in the MG is Sgt. Botwood.

A WARTIME POLICEMAN, PC Roy Baker, with his tin hat and gas mask.

THE TRAFFIC SECTION, West Sussex Constabulary c. 1938, outside the Section House, Kingsham Road. Back row, left to right: PCs J. Harvey, J. Lemm, L. Nicholls, D. Lovell, ? Goodbody. Front row: PC Cook, Sgt. Ball, Insp. McKneown, Sgt. Carter, Sgt. Kennett.

SECTION FOURTEEN

Music

Musical events, clubs and societies have been established in the city for many years. Liszt is among those to have performed at the Assembly Rooms. Others include the local amateur operatic society, since 1908, the music clubs, the choir of the Cathedral and the now one-hundred-year-old amateur orchestral society. Bands regularly played in the parks in the summer and musical concerts continue with performances in the Festival Theatre and at the annual Chichester festivities.

ROYAL SUSSEX REGIMENT BANDSMEN.

CORN EXCHANGE,
CHICHESTER.

WEDNESDAY, JAN. 18th,
AT 8.15 P.M., and
THURSDAY, JAN. 19th, 1911
AT 3 P.M., and 8.15 P.M.,

THE CHICHESTER AMATEUR OPERATIC SOCIETY
(President—The Right Hon. the Countess of March)

Will present (by kind permission of Mrs. D'Oyly Carte), Gilbert & Sullivan's Original Comic Opera, "The

PIRATES OF ENZANCE,'

Or "THE SLAVE OF DUTY,"
In Aid of Chichester Infirmary.

CASTE.

Major General Stanley	Mr. W. T. COLE.
The Pirate King	Mr. REGINALD STEWART.
Samuel (His Lieutenant)	Mr. JACK PETRIE.
Frederick (The Pirate Apprentice)	Mr. ROBERT MARLEY.
Sergeant of Police	Mr. ERN MILES.
Mabel	Miss CLARE LILLYWHITE.
Edith ⎱ General Stanley's	Mrs. REGINALD STEWART.
Kate ⎰ Daughters.	Mrs. WILL. SINDEN.
Isabel	Miss DOROTHY KERWOOD.
Ruth (Pirate Maid of all Work)	Miss KATRINE ST. CLAIR.

CHORUS of Pirates, Police, General Stanley's Daughters: Mesdames G. T. Apps, W. V. Cook, H. R. Cutten, R. W. Dawtrey, A. T. Humphry, W. H. Rands, R. F. Weller; Misses R. Charge, M. A. Dix, E. Hall, J. Hooper, F. Hooper, D. Howard, D. Kimbell, E. Lake, D. Lake, H. Napper, M. Purchase, E. Willis, N. Willis; Messrs. A. H. Caiger, L. Chaffer, H. Cresswell, C. W. Daughtry, H. H. Dyer, L. Evans, H. Furniss, C. Hall, W. Jones, E. H. Lake, T. F. Lummus, F. H. Manners, W. H. Rands, W. Whiteside, W. G. Willis.

FULL ORCHESTRA.

ACT I.	.. ..	A Rocky Seashore on the Coast of Cornwall.
ACT II.	.. ..	Ruined Chapel by Moonlight.

Hon. Conductor...MR. H. BRODIE.   Hon. Stage Manager...MR. EDGAR WARD. Hon. Secretary ... ... (23, South St., Chichester) MR. REG. B. STEWART. Costumes, Wigs, Scenes and Effects, by Drury. Electric Lighting by Messrs. Strange & Son, Ltd., Chichester. Limelight Effects by Messrs. R. W. Dawtrey and G. Kemp.

Evening Performances: Doors open at 7.45; Early Door 7.30.
Matinee: Doors open at 2.30; Early Doors, 2.15.
Early Doors at all Performances 6d. extra to Unreserved Seats. Tickets purchased before dates of Performances admit to early doors without extra charge.

Prices of Admission: Matinee: Reserved Seats 5s. & 3s.; Unreserved Seats 2s.; Admission 1s.
Evenings: Reserved Seats, 4s. & 3s.; Unreserved 2s.; Admission 1s.
Carriages at 5 p.m. and 10.15 p.m.

Seats booked at Pillow & Sons, The Cross, Chichester, where Plans of the Hall may be seen

T. G. Willis & Co., Printers, 21, East Street, Chichester.

PLAYBILL AND PHOTOGRAPHS OF THE CAST of the Chichester Amateur Operatic Society's first production which took place at the Corn Exchange in East Street, on 18 and 19 January 1911. Many of the names are of old Chichester families: Cutten, Charge, Hooper, Kimbell, Napper and Purchase.

THE BAND OF THE ROYAL SUSSEX REGIMENT marching down South Street from the Cross c. 1926–30. Note the cinema, The Picturedrome, forerunner of the Plaza, later the Odeon.

SOMERSTOWN FIFE AND DRUM BAND in Oaklands Park about 1900. The band was formed in 1895. In 1908 the secretary was Mr Elderton and its headquarters was The Beehive in Somerstown.

THE CHICHESTER CITY BAND in 1927, when they celebrated forty years of existence. In 1927 the bandmaster was Mr E. Shepherd, and during the summer the band played regularly in the parks every Wednesday and alternate Sundays. Thomas Heasman (standing middle row, fourth from left) usually played the cornet or the euphonium.

MISS DOROTHY COMBES of Green Lane in costume as the Lavender Girl in the Operatic Society production of the *Yeoman of the Guard*.

THE COMBES FAMILY OF GREEN LANE out for a country walk in the early 1900s. Mrs Cheetham, the grandmother in black, is pushing the pram with Sidney inside. The other babies are Bill and Jack. On the right are Annie Combes, daughter of Mrs Cheetham and Dorothy Combes (later Greenfield).

BONNETS FOR THE COMBES BABIES in their pram c. 1905.

A PARTY FOR MEMBERS OF THE BLIND CLUB in the early 1950s. Sidney Combes, in the white hat, is with Norman Smith, later vicar of Chidham.

HANDBELL RINGERS at the Blind Club in the 1950s. On the left are Miss Fry with Miss Downer standing next to Sid Combes.

ACKNOWLEDGEMENTS

Norman Reynolds ● Mervyn Cutten ● Chichester District Museum (Curator Miss Rosemary Gilmour) ● Chichester Amateur Operatic Society Norman Pritchard ● Alan Lambert ● Archie Greenshields ● Raymond Dobson Miss Grace Howard ● the Dean and Chapter of Chichester Cathedral (particularly Mrs Hobbs) ● Shippam's Ltd ● Peter Dunnaway ● Peter Fielder ● Roy Baker Betty Blyth ● Ere Featherstone

(Special thanks to Mervyn Cutten for his collection of material on Chichester including St Pancras Corporation, and to the staff of the Chichester District Musuem.)